Mark at Work

The Bible Reading Fellowship was founded
'to encourage the systematic and
intelligent reading of the Bible, to emphasize its
spiritual message and to take advantage of
new light shed on Holy Scripture'.

Over the years the Fellowship has proved
a trustworthy guide for those who want an open,
informed and contemporary approach to the Bible.
It retains a sense of the unique
authority of Scripture as a prime means
by which God communicates.

As an ecumenical organization, the
Fellowship embraces all Christian traditions and
its readers are to be found in most parts of the world.
It remains very much alive
to changes in attitudes, needs and situations
and produces material to meet them.

Write or call now for full list of publications.

The Bible Reading Fellowship

St Michael's House	P.O. Box M	All Saints Parish
2 Elizabeth Street	Winter Park	P.O. Box 328
London SW1W 9RQ	Florida 32790	Dickson ACT 2602
	USA	Australia

MARK AT WORK

John D. Davies
and
John J. Vincent

the bible reading fellowship

The authors' royalties from the sale of this book
will be used for the work of the Urban Theology
Unit, Sheffield.

First published 1986

© BRF 1986

The Bible Reading Fellowship
St Michael's House
2 Elizabeth Street
London SW1W 9RQ

Cover design: Joy Napper
Cover Bible: Good News Bible © American Bible Society 1976

British Library Cataloguing in Publication Data

Davies, John D.
  Mark at work.
  1.   Bible. N.T. Mark—Commentaries
  I. Title.   II. Vincent, John J.   III Bible Reading Fellowship
  226'.307   BS2585.3

ISBN 0–900164–68–9

Designed and printed by Bocardo Press Limited, Oxford

CONTENTS

Affectionately dedicated
to the memory of
Alan T. Dale

PREFACE

Mark at Work is based on three discoveries, which we want to share.

First, the discovery that we get more out of the Gospel when we read it as its first readers did — with our own current concerns and problems in our minds. It's best to start where we are — not where we might imagine New Testament people were. If Mark is to work on us, we have to be honest about who we are, and why we do what we do.

Second, the discovery that the Gospel will come back at us. It is quite able to bring its own perspectives, concerns and challenges. It will do battle with us. It will take us seriously, but then knock us off our guard. Through us, Mark will get to work in our world, our churches and our local communities, with some revolutionary ways of doing everything.

Third, the discovery that the Gospel has to be learned from each other. Our testimony is that everyone is a Bible interpreter. We have discovered that the best way to help people is to be enablers. We are not the experts — though we do confess to an inordinate fascination with Mark's Gospel, which we hope comes through! This book records ways we have found exciting and enabling, whereby others have got Mark working for them.

These approaches to Mark's Gospel began like this.

A group of us came together at the Urban Theology Unit in Sheffield at Easter 1973, to read the Gospel. As we did so, we developed some simple ways of asking questions to the text, and expecting the text to ask questions of us. Since then, among UTU people, at the Selly Oak Colleges, in churches, in adult and youth and student conferences and in groups of clergy and ministers, and sometimes in sermons and addresses, Mark has gone on being 'at work' among us.

We are still very much at the learning stage ourselves. Further illuminations constantly come from new groups. But the time is ripe for us to bring others in. Hence this book. It catches our work in midflow. There seem to be so many who find themselves coming alive through looking at the Gospel in these ways, or for whom the Gospel has come newly alive by their means, that we felt that we must try to share them more widely.

The methods are simple enough, once you get the hang of them. But the reader will derive most benefit from this book, not simply by reading it straight through, but by taking time, by experimenting with it. We hope that it may be of some value to preachers digging for sermons and to students researching texts: but, primarily and especially, we want to help the Gospel to be let loose among people who will study it together in a disciplined and expectant way, who will set aside a worthwhile period of time for it, who will insist not only on reading the Gospel but also reflecting on it, delving into it, working out its meaning for the corporate life and policy of the local church, acting it out and doing new gospel-events in their world — and who will then follow this up by report and further study.

It is just this sort of 'Work on the Word' which produced our Gospels as we now have them; and precisely this sort of work is needed now, to get the Gospel going again as a power for change in our lives today. So we call this book MARK AT WORK. We want to encourage and help people to put Mark to work in our present situations, to let his message have effect in our church and society, to explore ways in which his story can serve those who in these days are workers for God's realm. This was what Mark wrote his Gospel for, in the first century. We believe this is the way to use it today.

And we want to stress that, if there is any truth in the message which Mark presents, it must be a truth for the world in our ordinary work. It is not a truth limited to the narrow interests of religion or church-structure; it is a truth which is discovered in the experiences of struggle and conflict of interest, of social and personal disorder, in which Mark shows us a Christ most characteristically at work.

We have represented our methods in a variety of approaches and a mixture of styles. Sometimes, we give only outlines, sometimes a detailed exposition. We have no intention of offering a complete and systematic commentary on the whole text; all we try to do is to offer some representative samples of how our approaches can work, so that those who use the book can go on and work on the rest of the text themselves. We have tried to offer something on each of the major sections of Mark; but, for a group of people who try to work with this book, we say that the most important part of the study is what we have *not* written!

The book represents our joint work, even though we first drafted the chapters individually. Where we have quoted Mark, we have often used our own translations. We would encourage those who use this book to study it in conjunction with a modern English translation like the Revised Standard Version — the Common Bible — or the Good News Bible, or some other contemporary version. The first part of Alan T. Dale's *New World* has most of Mark's Gospel, in sequence.

Two names are on the title-page. Alan T. Dale worked with us with characteristic enthusiasm, commitment and insight, until his death in Spring 1979. Chapters 14 and 16 especially owe much to him. This volume, like his Memorial Library at UTU, will be a reminder of what we and so many others owe to him.

John D. Davies
John J. Vincent

PART ONE

Approaches

1. Why We Study the Gospels

THE SECOND CHRISTIANS

We are in the age of the second Christians.

The first Christians were the people who were affected by Jesus directly, and who recognized something of the truth about him. A mixed group they were. For instance, there was a junior officer of a colonial army of occupation, whose duties included the supervision of crucifixions. This centurion was the first person to recognize the crucified Son of God (Mark 15:33). In this sense, he was one of the first Christians. Then there was the first person to recognize the risen Christ, a person who, on account of being female, would not be accepted as a credible witness in a contemporary court of law: Mary Magdalene also was one of the first Christians (Mark 16:1; Luke 8:2). Then there were the people whom Jesus himself called, an unpromising collection of men with no great education or social prestige, who were consistent only in misunderstanding and reliable only for getting in the way (e.g. Mark 1:16–20; 9:33–35; 10:13–14). The disciples also were the first Christians. On the evidence given by this tiny handful of improbable people, countless millions of us have been convinced about the meaning of Jesus.

Soon, another group of Christians came into being — the second Christians. They were convinced by the message brought by the first Christians. They committed themselves to the new Kingdom which Jesus had announced; but they heard of this kingdom through the message of the first Christians, not directly from Jesus himself. And in other ways their situation was different: most of the second Christians were not living in Jerusalem or Galilee; their problems did not centre around the complaints of Jewish temple-officials and local nationalists. They were living in areas like Corinth, Rome, Ephesus and Antioch; there most people were Gentiles. Some of their main problems were to work out the new relationship between Jew and Gentile, the right attitude to the authority of the Roman Emperor, the right response to pagan ways of thinking and behaving.

These 'Second Christians' were convinced that Jesus was with them, as their Master and source of truth. He was with them as much as he had been with the first Christians. Nobody tried to choose a *successor* to Jesus! But what about the stories which the first Christians remembered, about the activities of Jesus in Galilee and Judaea? What use were they? The 'Second Christians' faced new questions, questions to which the stories of Jesus could give no answer because Jesus had never faced them. Jesus had never given an answer to such questions as 'Should Jews and Gentiles eat together?' or 'Can we eat food that has been sacrificed to idols?' Such questions had not occurred in Jesus' experience. So, for these 'second Christians', there was not much point in asking 'What did Jesus say?' But they could ask 'What is the Spirit of Jesus trying to say to us now?' And so they were led to a new obedience in unprecedented situations. When that happened, they found that the older stories of Jesus were, after all, worth remembering and re-telling; they discovered the connections between what God had been doing in Jesus and what God was seeking to do through them in their new situations. So they treasured and recorded these stories: they needed the stories of the past in order to interpret and to respond to the demands of the present.

Now we are in this year of ours and in this place of ours. Here and now, we also are groups of 'second Christians'. We are in the same situation, fundamentally, as the 'second Christians' in Corinth or Antioch. We, like them, face new questions, questions which cannot simply be answered by asking 'What did Jesus say?' We are the early Church for 1986. No one has ever been here before us.

So we need the same approach as those 'second Christians' of 1900 years ago. We seek to know what our Christian obedience means in our unprecedented situations. Like them, we have to start with the demand of our own situation, we discover connections between it and the stories of Jesus, and we are given a clearer understanding of the action or response which God seeks to make through us in our world.

This is why we read the Gospels. This is the only reason. The Gospels are not intended to give us mere information, or facts about days gone by, or an uplifting spiritual experience, or a design for social improvement. The Gospels were written in response to the Church's need, as it struggled to be a missionary community committed to the programme of Christ's Kingdom. The New Testament is all about the transformation of persons, of society, of the universe. It is about Christ's programme of remaking creation so that it becomes true to the mind and purpose of the Creator. To treat it merely as an object of historical or literary study, or as a source of individual comfort, is to misuse it, to bend it from its purpose: it is like using a chisel for a screwdriver — it's bound to make a mess. The Gospels start to make sense when they are picked up by a group of people who want to be a missionary community. Only a cook really *understands* ovens: other people may get to know a lot of facts about them; but to understand you have to use. Only a missionary Christian can really *understand* the Gospels. This small book is offered to people who want to be part of the Christian movement, putting the Gospel story to work.

This book, we hope, will be of most interest to small groups of Christians who wish to test out and to transform their church practice and policy in the light of the stories of the Gospel. We believe that to use the stories in this way is to be faithful to the original purpose of the gospel-writers. The Christian community refers to itself as the Body of Christ. A body is a person acting, speaking, experiencing. The Body of Christ is Christ acting, speaking, experiencing, making gospel-events, in the days of the New Testament people and in our own day. The Gospels are the record of the words, the actions, the experiences and the suffering of Jesus: they tell us what God looked like, incarnate in the person of Jesus. In the Christian community, the Body of Christ, God seeks to continue that word, action, experience and suffering in our own day.

So, in practical terms, we may expect and pray to get two things from our work of Gospel-study:

1. We can see what God's action is like in the world; and from this we can get mandates, priorities, guidelines for our programme as a Christian group — healing, proclaiming, confronting, compassion-ing.

2. We can see the effects to which obedience to the Kingdom leads: we can see what God suffers in the world in the person of Jesus. From this we gain resources for interpreting and coping with the effects of our own work — the misunderstandings, conflicts of interest, clashes with authority, periods of storm, darkness and delay. Because Christ is risen, the members of his Body can face the carrying of the cross after him.

So this is the summary of our purpose in studying the Gospels: to seek guidelines for our programme in the Christian movement, and to gain encouragement in coping with the efforts and results of our programme.

2. How We Study the Gospels

WAYS INTO GOSPEL STUDY

1. Reading the whole story.

Before you start work in a study-group, and before you attend to any particular section of the Gospel-story, read the whole text of the Gospel. Read the Gospel of Mark right through from beginning to end — preferably in one sitting. It will take you perhaps an hour and a half. Use any version, Good News, Revised Standard, New English Bible, J.B. Phillips, William Barclay or Alan Dale's 'New World' part 1.

Even if you think that you know the whole story well, read it straight through. You will probably find that you know some parts better than others: you will need to realize how the well-known parts fit into the whole.

It is good to have a copy which you can put marks in as you go along:

 Put a star against something which you think is specially important.

 Put a question mark against something which puzzles you.

 Draw a little light-bulb against something which strikes you as new illumination.

 Put a cross against something which seems to be wrong or offensive to you.
And so on.

If possible, do this in partnership with another person. Then when you have both read through the text of the Gospel, you can share some of your immediate impressions.

A PROGRAMME FOR STUDYING A PASSAGE
(If you like diagrams, this page may help you. If not, skip it!)

At its simplest, any Bible-study has to involve three elements:
    imagining;
    thinking;
    deciding.
Also, it inevitably involves looking back on the past; so we could describe it as a kind of loop-movement:

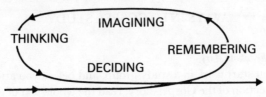

We study the Bible to help us to sort out plans and priorities. This sort of aim — whether in Bible-study or in anything else — involves a similar kind of loop as we look at the past and plan for the future.

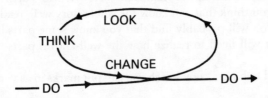

We take this kind of pattern, and apply it to the study of a story in the Gospel. First, we use our imagination to see connections between the situation in the Gospel and our own situation (Snaps); then we think objectively about the meaning of the text (Studies); then we move towards the future and discover the decisions which are suggested for our future work, in the light of our study (Spin-offs).

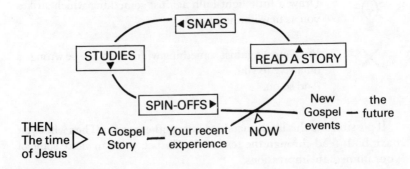

2. Studying a passage.

In most of this book, we are concerned with studying specific passages. We have deliberately not set out to write a full commentary: we have merely taken a few representative or specimen passages, to show the following method at work. Whatever the type of passage, the study should in principle have the following ingredients.

i. Starting where we are.

On the diagram, we are at the point marked 'NOW'. We are the people we are, at the point in time which is *now*, at the position which is *here*. We are on a line of experience. Behind us is our own immediate past, and also behind us is the history of the whole Christian movement. Our task is to go on making that history, to be people through whom God continues to make gospel-actions. But, at this point marked 'NOW', we take time off from our task in order to go back to our sources and check our priorities. We move off the line of experience, so as to reflect on our own immediate experience and on the experience of the first members of our movement. So we pick up our copy of the Gospel.

ii. Reading a Story.

Start with a story, with one of the episodes in the Gospel narrative. Before you get into technicalities, be *yourself*. What catches your interest in the story? What 'clicks' with you, with your experience or imagination? Whom do you identify with? And why? This is about *you*. At this point, you can't be wrong — even if you are technically misunderstanding the text. Before worrying about misunderstandings, claim the story as *yours*. Catch the story from your own point of view. Tell it to someone else, with your particular slant.

iii. Snaps.

By a 'snap' we mean the first impression, the snapshot. Snap — the two similar cards. Snap — the connector of two electric cables. 'Snaps' make connections between us, as we are, and the story. Snaps work in our *imaginations*.

For example, you might take Mark 2:1–12, the first 'big' story in Mark's Gospel. You might identify with one or other of the characters in the story. 'I feel like Jesus — always being interrupted'; 'I think I'm a scribe, always picking holes in other people'; 'I know what it's like to be flat on my back waiting for help' — said by a miner who recalled being trapped in a rock-fall; 'I feel like the roof — people just knock holes in me'. And so on.

STUDIES

iv. Studies.

Then we need to start a more objective search. What is going on in the story? What is happening to people and why? This is the point where you need a bit of *specialist knowledge*, for this is where it is quite possible to get the story wrong or (more likely) to fail to see points which would be clear to Mark and his readers. For instance, you may need to find out more about the Old Testament background, or the social, political and economic conditions of Jesus' day, or the living problems of the church for which Mark wrote. This is where you may have to get your books out (see list at the end of this book), to consult your minister, to adjourn your meeting till next time and delegate one of your members to do some research for you.

But the 'studies' phase is not necessarily bookwork. Build on the 'identifications' you have already made. If you are doing this with others, divide your group into little teams around the characters which interest you.

To continue our example of Mark 2:1–12, these teams could be Jesus, the bearers, the crowd, the patient, the scribes. In each team, ask 'What is happening to us? What are our goals and our problems?' — and the 'we' is not you as a group of readers or church members but you in the role of Jesus, the bearers, etc. Don't say, 'I think the scribes have problem X' but 'I am a scribe and as such I have problem X'. Then let each team send a couple of delegates to the team that is causing their problems and face them with it: or let each team send to the team to which they are causing problems and ask 'What is the problem that I am causing you?' Then the issues in this complex story can be faced in pairs of roles. For instance, the paralysed man, by his presence, causes problems to the crowd or congregation, for whom he is an interruption. The crowd or congregation is a problem to the bearers. The bearers present a problem to Jesus. Jesus is a problem to the scribes. The scribes are a problem to the paralysed man. What is motivating these groups of people? How do they express their needs and attitudes? What are their responses?

Very many stories of Mark are stories of conflict between various interest-groups. Each of these interest-groups has some legitimacy, but Christ's presence tends to polarize these interests into faith and anti-faith.

Go for the roles, not for individual character-analysis. Mark does not ask us to go in for deep psychological speculation. Individual characters belong uniquely to their own context. People in their roles are transferable; we can find them in our own context. So, for instance, when we read that Jesus was 'indignant' about the condition of a leper (Mark 1:40–45 — this is the best translation of the original words), we don't speculate about what was so specially wrong with this particular leper. We ask, Who is the leper for us, in our society today? Who is fulfilling the role of 'leper'? What does a Jesus-following church do in order to carry on Jesus' work towards such people? If we do this honestly, we may well find that we see more clearly why Jesus was 'indignant'.

In our 'studies' phase, we are seeing two things at once. We are seeing an action or saying of Jesus. And we are seeing something of the impact or effect which the story made on the gospel-writer Mark. We see that it is a story which he and his community remembered and treasured and valued so much that it got written down. Only a tiny fraction of the things that Jesus said and did were so significant to the Christian community. So it's useful to ask what was so special about the particular story we are studying. How did it help Mark's community to face up to their problems? So, Mark is, in a sense, another character represented on the printed page you are reading. If your group breaks into little teams to get into the role of the different characters of the story, don't forget to include Mark. Let a team try to think out why Mark found the story worth remembering and recording for his church. This will help you to discover meaning in the story for your contemporary situation.

SPIN-OFFS

v. Spin-offs.

Then we turn back from our 'studies' and get into the direction of our *present life*. What are the '*Spin-offs*'? What are the mandates, implications, applications? What effect is this Bible-study going to have on your church's programme? Does it support you, criticize you, offer you new suggestions for action? Does it help you to cope with the effects of your gospel-programme? Does it direct you towards gospel-activity in your neighbourhood?

At this point, no one from outside your situation can tell you what is right for you. The most that anyone else can do is to tell you stories of how the gospel-material has worked out elsewhere.

This moment of change of direction is, in many ways, the most important moment of the whole Bible-study. Your seriousness at this point will make all the difference; it will show whether you are interested in merely having a pleasant discussion, or whether you are really in business with the policies of Jesus. You may well find that there are all sorts of pressures, conscious and sub-conscious, to delay or omit this shift of direction. It is a change of mood and a change of skill. You have to move, perhaps with some pain, from the intellectual pursuits of 'there and then' into decision-making for the 'here and now' — and you may well find that you run into real-life conflicts of interest. So don't leave this change of direction until too late in your meeting. You must change from being a story-reader into being a story-maker.

Before there can be a story to tell, it has to be acted out; and that new action is your task. You go on to work out, in action, the roles that you have been examining.

1. You and your church are part of the needy world that Christ heals and nourishes. In what ways are you needing Christ's healing for your paralysis, your leprosy, your demon-possession, your hunger?
2. You and your church are part of the disciple-community which Christ teaches, and which so often misunderstands and obstructs. Where and how are you failing to co-operate with him and to learn from him? What has he been teaching you in the last year or two?
3. You and your church are part of the rejoicing crowd which has an eye and a song for the signs of God's love in the world. What is God doing in your bit of the world, and how are you celebrating it?
4. Above all, you are the Body of Christ himself; through you, God wishes to continue the gospel-events once typically acted out by Jesus of Nazareth. What is God trying to do for his world through your particular group or church?

PART TWO

Sequences

3. Introduction

How and why Mark put his book together in the way he did is a source of endless discussion.

Some people think that the stories are in more or less chronological order. Some think that they were already side by side in written material to which Mark had access. Some think that Mark linked his various pieces in groups because they had common themes. Some think that Mark arranged it all very carefully to develop certain major themes. Some think that he put passages together because they had specific words or phrases in common.

Possibly, Mark at times did all of these. Certainly, we can discover a whole series of 'linking-passages', which Mark introduced between the various pieces he had to deal with. Often these 'linking-passages' are only a few words, introduced by such words as 'immediately', or 'when he had. . .' or 'then'.

Yet, it is striking how certain passages do 'hang together', and make most sense in the light of the pieces which precede and follow them. The chapter divisions are not the creation of Mark himself, of course; but sometimes a chapter gives a 'sequence' which seems to invite one to say, 'Isn't that so like my own experience, when one thing follows another, or illuminates another, or corrects another?'

So, in the following section, we invite you to read a few 'Sequences', and to ask whether they light up your own life as they did the lives of the early Christians.

4. Getting a Movement Going

MARK 1: PART 1

Who has got a story of the beginning of some project? It doesn't matter what sort — it could be a shop, a news-sheet, a Sunday School, a fishing club, a scheme for child-minding.

What has to happen, if anything is to get going?

Someone has to have a sense of need, a vision.

Whoever is going to start the scheme needs to know the potential 'market', the local area.

Whoever is going to lead the scheme needs to be able to 'sell' it, and to be able to cope with disappointment.

The leader needs to think the idea through and have some idea of the implications and consequences — inspiration is fine but it isn't enough!

Often, it's best to start with people who aren't too tied up with lots of other commitments.

If the scheme is to succeed, those involved need to feel that they have a real job to do: they need to have a purpose, a goal, a programme.

What else?

STUDIES

So we have recognized some of the things which must happen in starting a movement. Some of these will be necessary in starting almost any kind of enterprise; and we can find them in the specific movement started by Jesus.

For this first stage, we concentrate on Mark 1:1–20.

Movements in general	Jesus' movement
(a) THE LEADER	
i. Identification with existing set-up: knowing the area.	Involvement in John the Baptist's programme, submission to his ministry. (1–9)
ii. Leader has to have personal confidence.	Jesus is affirmed as 'my beloved Son'. (11)
iii. Leader has to work out his ideas, and has to learn to cope with isolation.	Jesus goes into the desert, to be tempted. (12)
(b) THE SITUATION	
iv. Starting where there is a need, where there is an opening, on the frontier.	Into Galilee. (14)
v. An appropriate moment, when a new opportunity arises.	After John's arrest. (14)
(c) THE MANIFESTO	
vi. Statement of a new possibility or opportunity.	The Kingdom of God is at hand.
vii. People challenged to take advantage of new options.	Repent: a new chance! Away with complacency! (15)
viii. Demand for commitment, signing people up.	Trust yourself to the Good News. (15)

Movements in general	Jesus' movement
(d) **THE MOVEMENT**	
ix. A movement which people can join.	Come with me. (17)
x. The offer of work and roles.	I will make you fishers of men. (17)
xi. Choosing people who are able to take up new commitments.	They left their nets. (18, 20)
xii. Formation of a committed working team.	They followed him. (18, 20)

We can find the basic outline of this process in the starting of almost any kind of movement or project, from a stamp club to the National Front. Thus, in the 'green' or anti-nuclear movement today, many people individually pass through the stages of decision (a 'conscientization' — getting to see things as they really are) represented by i, ii and iii. They then (iv) look at their situation and (v) find the right time. The campaign then gets going with (vi) a declaration of a new pollution-free, ecologically sound world, (vii) a demand that total lifestyle change is necessary, (viii) complete trust in the new possibility of a non-nuclear and 'green' world, (ix) an invitation to join a specific group of people — the campaigners — and (x) an expectation that everyone will be involved in carrying on the mission. Finally, (xi) the 'nets' of an irrelevant and superseded technological society are left behind, and (xii) one is committed to the movement.

So, in this sequence in Mark, we find guidelines for the early stages of a movement. These features will need to have a place in the work of Jesus' followers — in first-century Rome or in twentieth-century Britain. So we look at these features in more detail: the numbers refer to the items in the sequence above.

i. Jesus starts where people are. He joins a movement which is already in being. He becomes part of the contemporary scene. He belongs. But he doesn't join any old movement. There were several other movements and pressure-groups on offer at the time. Jesus joined John's movement. It was unlike other movements, because John appealed to ordinary people, to the peasants, to the poor, rather than to a religious or paramilitary power-base. Also, it was different because John insisted that God required the *whole* of society to be changed, whereas other movements assumed that the blame for all problems could be put on someone else — the colonial overlords, the 'sinners', the masses. So the Jesus-movement starts by finding the people who are 'hungry for change', *and* are willing to be changed themselves.

ii, iii. The sense of some kind of *personal call*, some sort of recognition of one's authority and right to take action. This is the 'high' point which is immediately followed by the driving off into the desert. In the Department of Mission at the Selly Oak Colleges in Birmingham, at the Urban Theology Unit at Sheffield, and in training events up and down the country, the authors constantly see this happening with all kinds of people who feel a call to mission overseas or in Britain. Time and again, the process of call or selection and getting one's vocation clear is followed immediately by a testing in isolation, a removal of landmarks, a desert experience of some sort. This may happen either immediately after the clarification of one's vocation, or when one starts preparing for the unknown, or arrives in the new place to get going. Mark gets the element of 'desert' across, without all the agenda represented by the temptation stories in the other gospels. The main point of the desert is not a packed agenda but sheer emptiness.

iv. Jesus starts on the *frontier*. If you do not start on the frontier, if you start in the metropolitan centre, you confirm the existing power-systems of geography, culture and control. The frontiers of society are often the crucial places to begin.

And Jesus starts in Galilee with unpowerful, provincial people. Again, unless you start with those who do not have power, rather than at the centres of power, you merely confirm the oppressive forces within society.

v. In 'Starting a Movement', there is always something like 'Waiting for the Appropriate Moments'. In the case of Jesus, it was the opportunity created by the police-action, in arresting John the Baptist and creating a kind of leadership-vacuum.

vi–xii. There is an alternative option given to the hitherto unrecognized person. To these uninfluential characters Jesus says: 'You are going to be fishers of men. Until now, you have been fishers of fish, but in my programme you will become people of social influence.' The disciple has to have the sense that 'before I go out to change the world, I am conscious that I have myself been changed'. This is exactly parallel to the process of Magnificat. 'Putting down the mighty from their seat' is a vision which begins in the first person singular. Everything begins with the sense that I, as a totally disadvantaged and unrecognized person, have suddenly been given status (Luke 1:46–55).

SPIN-OFFS

1. In your local community, now, what signs are there that you are being called to start something new?

2. Are you, in some way, at a 'frontier', or 'on the fringe'?

3. What sort of people will you start with?

4. What sort of qualifications are required for new followers or workers for Christ?

5. A Day in the Life of Jesus

MARK 1: PART 2

1. Divide your day, up till now, into sections:
   How many different things have happened to you?
   How many stories have you got to tell?

2. How far has your day worked out as you originally planned?

3. Who were the decisive people who made a difference to your plans?

Chapter one really is an *exhausting* chapter. Verses 21 to 34 describe the events of a single day, taken up first thing the next morning (35) with an attempt by Jesus to get some quiet. But his disciples find him and tell him that people are looking for him (36–37), to which he replies by saying that he must not stay in one place (38). He is not simply 'available', always ready to respond to people's needs and demands. He has a programme and an agenda of his own. He disappoints those who try to tell him his job. He is also setting a pattern for his disciples: they, too, had to keep on the move, and 'leave those parts' (6:10).

So, already in Mark's story, we are invited to think of the disciples' work and the work of Jesus in the same way. His work is a key to their work. His movement is the movement in which they must share.

How does this relate to a settled congregation, the 'second Christians' of AD 60 or 1986? It has recently been suggested that Mark is a book for travelling preachers. People are called to leave all and follow (1:16–20; 2:13–14), to be prepared to go on with Jesus even when local people want to keep them or him (38). To be a disciple is to be a person who gets up and goes.

So, even the little settled congregation in Rome or Wigan has to expect to be responding to calls. This obviously doesn't mean everybody all the time. But there has to be kingdom-preaching and kingdom-acting, and those in more 'static' roles have to be ready to move if necessary — or to support others called to move.

The whole of chapter one can be looked at from the point of view of the way Christians have to do their work, carry out their mission, or extend the movement of the Kingdom of God.

We suggest that you now go back to the chapter, and read it again — noting (1) the things that Jesus does, as events concerning his character and significance, and (2) the things that we might be called to get into, if we take the events of the story seriously. The first list we shall call 'Marks of Jesus' — things we notice about him in the stories. The second list we call 'Strategies for Us' — things we might find ourselves doing (not all at once!) as we serve his movement.

JESUS' WORK AND OURS		
verses	**Marks of Jesus** **Jesus is:**	**Strategies For Us** **Christian work is:**
1–8	The one who is greater than Prophet or Revivalist, already present but not yet recognized.	Pointing to Jesus already present but not yet properly acknowledged.
9–11	Baptised into John's movement, affirmed by the Holy Spirit and the Father's voice.	Joining existing pressure-groups, but with a new confidence and authority.
12–13	Driven into isolation, struggling with the unholy spirit.	Agonizing about vocation, methods, priorities, without visible companionship.

JESUS' WORK AND OURS

verses	Marks of Jesus Jesus is:	Strategies For Us Christian work is:
14–15	Advertising a new opportunity, announcing God's authority and jurisdiction.	Telling about the true ownership of the world, the true authority over it, demanding that people recognize this and change.
16–20	Choosing and forming a new community.	Forming a team based on Christ's call.
21–22	Claiming recognition for his authority as teacher.	Demanding recognition for truth of message, rather than for the authority of the religious system.
23–24	Recognized by threatened hostile forces.	First recognized by threatened enemies, not by religious allies.
25–28	The attacker and destroyer of powers which ravage God's creation.	Identifying and attacking the opponents of God's order.
29–31	One who cares about private and personal suffering, as well as for public confrontation.	Caring for fellow-workers and for unglamorous needs which get no publicity.
32–34	Available to human need.	Being on the spot where need is great.
35	One who maintains his relationship in prayer.	Prayer, keeping the priority of relationship with God.
36–39	In demand, but keeping control of his own agenda.	Keeping one's own priorities, not getting trapped by a fan-club.
40–45	Responding to the need of an outcast, accepting contamination.	Being willing to pay the price for caring for unpopular people.

SPIN-OFFS

What things could you get into if you followed some of the hints in the list of Jesus' Work and Ours?

FOR CHRISTIAN WORKERS

Do you need to find a place where you can become a missionary, a place where there are no Christians? One reason why Islam rather than Christianity conquered North Africa was that the Christians were 'residential' whereas Moslems were travellers. We tend to discount nomads, wandering tribes. They don't fit into the plans and bureaucracies of the 'normal' settled people. But a recent UN survey has shown that there are vast areas of country which should be used say every six years or so — rather than either farmed yearly or left as jungle or desert. Nomads are necessary — though they may be inconvenient for Church and State! How well do our British Churches relate to such groups as Travellers or Gypsies?

FOR INDIVIDUALS

Where are you up to in your participation in the twelve stages of the Movement of Jesus? What is the call for you? It is always difficult to leave where you are — security, home, loved ones, familiar surroundings, people who appreciate you. The call is sometimes negative — to 'opt out'. People sometimes 'opt out' of life — visit India, go in for non-productive work, 'flip-out'. The Gospel-call is to 'opt in' to God's movement, but that would mean to 'opt out' of other things.

FOR DISCIPLE GROUPS

John Wesley's travelling preachers were essentially 'itinerant'. They had to keep on the move. A preacher might only 'travel' for two or three years, then return home to his own family and job, for a rest. Even today, a Methodist minister is said to have 'travelled' for forty or whatever years of ministry. Wesley's first 'preaching places' were overnight, or two-three days, 'resting-places' as at the New Room in Bristol.

'Moving-on' is basic to any Christian group. This is true for the early Church. The more widely the pattern of 'residential' Christian groups is repeated, the more it is necessary for people to be prepared to keep 'on the move' into new kingdom-projects or kingdom-announcement. People need to 'move on', in mental and occupational and vocational ways, as well as geographically.

What items might you move on to, in any of our lists for Mark 1?

6. A Movement in Mission

Once a movement has started, it gathers momentum. Chapter three indicates a sequence of events that we can study, as we try to 'get going' our own efforts as Christians.

Here, we do well to remember what was said in the first chapter about our being the 'second Christians'. The Gospel was written by people thirty years or so after Jesus started the Movement with his disciples in Galilee. So the way the Gospel is written reflects not only the Movement in Jesus' day in AD 30, but also the Movement in AD 60 or 70. Also, we are not the first 'second Christians' to read the Gospel. We read it remembering what other Christians in other times before us have made of it for the Movement in their day. The 'snap' process was already happening in the New Testament.

So, we can look for a number of things about a story in the Gospel:

1. The precise context in the ministry of Jesus, if we can know it. What started the story off?

2. The meaning of the stories for Mark himself, and for his readers. What did it mean then?

3. Mark's context for the story within his total Gospel. Why is the story told here, and this way?

4. Representative contexts in the subsequent history of the Church. What has it motivated? What people lived out this story?

Let us see how this works out in the story of a Movement in Mission, in Mark 3. Here we are given a series of typical features of this fairly early stage of a movement.

First of all, the apostle or missionary appears, and some kind of 'happening' takes place (vv. 1–6). Then, a crowd of interested people follow the apostle/missionary (vv. 7–12), and a debate ensues as to the significance of the happening (v. 11). Those who become allied to the apostle/missionary obtain a new commitment and status (vv. 13–19), a status which is embarrassing to their previous relationships (vv. 20–21), and family (vv. 31–35). The religious authorities object to the new commitment (vv. 22–30), and the disciples of the new movement become all the more committed because of the opposition of others (v. 35).

We can find this kind of sequence in the experience of many churches in mission situations. It is certainly there, for instance, in the mission situation which we find in other parts of the New Testament, where the Church is moving into pagan Gentile communities in places such as Corinth. We can set out the corresponding patterns like this:

Verses	The Story of Jesus' Day	The Story in the Early Church
1–2	Jesus in the synagogue, with his contemporaries and relatives, the synagogue ruler and officials, and some scribes.	Scene is set in a church gathering, in which some are of Jewish background, some pagan, some educated, some property-owners, some slaves, many illiterate.
3	Man with withered hand. Stand up!	A decisive gospel-happening takes place — a healing, conversion, etc.
4	Debate about Sabbath. How must we obey the Law?	Discipleship brings unprecedented questions. For Gentiles, can we eat meat sacrificed to idols? for instance.
8	Tyre and Sidon, Gentile countries, are included.	The mission reaches people outside, all the time — new groups, illiterate people, slaves, travelling salesmen, soldiers.
11	Unclean spirits alone proclaim Jesus as 'Son of God'.	Apostles' work brings confrontation with secular authority (e.g. in Philippi, Acts 16).

Verses	The Story of Jesus' Day	The Story in the Early Church
13–19	Choice and appointment of Twelve.	Central significance of small disciple-group.
20–21	Relatives think Jesus 'out of his mind'.	The divine looks 'abnormal'. How far can this go (cp. 1 Cor. 14:23)?
22–27	Scribes attack Jesus as Satan-possessed.	The apostle has to put up with complaints from the church, which even then, was becoming an 'institution' (cp. 2 Cor. 11:1–15).
28–30	Is it really God at work?	Is it really God at work?
31–35	'Here are my mother and my brothers' within the group.	Christ is making a new race. Our 'mother and brothers' no longer necessarily come from parental identity but from the new creation (cp. Gal. 3:26–28).
32	Crowd stands by hearing him.	Onlookers are not committed, but still listen.
35	Anyone who does the will of God is Jesus' relative.	Converts excluded by families find new relatives.

This pattern could be illustrated in stories of dramatic conversion throughout Christian history. For example, 200 years ago John Wesley would appear in a small town, would engage in preaching and debate ('happening'), would gather a crowd of interested persons, would then separate out a smaller group of 'class leaders', would have to deal with the problem of opposition on the part of those who had previously known the converts, and on the part of religious authorities. Finally, the interior life of the religious societies, their hymns, their testimonies, their internal discipline, etc. would confirm the converts in belonging to 'the new family'.

Similar stories could be told from the mission field today. Readers might look up a few stories.

STUDIES

THREE CAUTIONS

Our 'searches' or 'studies' are meant to take us deeper into the passage. This time, there are three cautionary words.

1. The Jesus Reference is Vital.

This is not a sociologically 'distinctive' pattern. It can be the pattern of any new, revolutionary, small movement, 'doing its thing', getting disciples despite official opposition, and causing rupture of existing systems (family, etc.). What is distinctive is the naming of the Name, and the repeating of the unique Christian message and action. There are, indeed, also false groups and false Christs (Mark 13:21–23); not everyone is what they claim to be, and not everyone is doing a gospel thing just because the sequence of gospel-like events is taking place. We must therefore apply the test of the Gospel about what is really happening there. What *fruits* are brought forth? This is a hard question, which has to be asked concerning both 'Christian' and non-Christian movements. The 'fruits' are forms of change which are in line with the priorities of the Kingdom of God — the divine rule which Jesus brings (see Matthew 11:2–6). These are gospel-happenings. And a further test of whether something is a true gospel-happening is whether it leads on to other gospel-happenings.

2. The Jesus Style is Vital.

A key element is the 'happening' which starts it all off. In Mark 3:1–6, the healing of the man with the withered hand is the decisive starting-point. The event is one which brings wholeness to a suffering person. There are a number of elements which we can look for:

(i) *A Gospel-Action*, in line with Jesus' liberating work of healing (vv. 1–3).

(ii) The event happens in a place where people have a *tradition, a social and cultural context*. This context gives a location for the gospel-action; it gives people ways to understand the gospel-action, but it is itself questioned and judged by the gospel-action, which shows up its limitations (vv. 1–4).

(iii) *Traditional categories cannot explain the gospel-action*; only Jesus' own explanation is possible (vv. 28–30).

(iv) *Acceptance by undesirables* (vv. 7–9).

Consequently, we are always looking for a 'happening' which has real gospel content. We need to build up a set of 'marks' whereby we can discern what is and what is not a gospel-event.

3. The language of demon-possession — is it vital?

In the Gospel story, to cast out demons means to liberate people from powers which threaten to destroy them and which make them unable to respond to the call to discipleship. For some of us now, language about demons can be an escape into an unreal world; it can help us to avoid facing the real evils in our own motives and in society. But, for others, the language about demons can be very useful and true; it can be a valid and dramatic way of saying that there is a whole range of things opposed to the Jesus things, which can best be labelled as demonic things. So use the demonic language if it helps you get hold of some reality which is 'possessing' you — but not as a way of avoiding challenges facing you. (On demons, see also later, p. 55.)

SPIN-OFFS

1. Where is the Movement of Jesus happening, catching on, producing new events or situations, making authorities sit up and take notice?

2. What happening that you could be in on, or precipitate, or act out, would have enough marks of the Gospel for it to initiate the gospel-sequence (rejection by powers, small group's loyalty, healing for others, etc.)?

7. A Movement's Inner Dynamic

MARK 4

Whom do we feel like?

1. Like *'those outside'* (v. 11)? The Parables are confusing. We don't get the point.

2. Like the *stony ground* (v. 16)? We've too much on already. It could be interesting. But only for an hour. It won't stand a chance. And if anything happens, a lot remain alienated! Jealousies creep in. Some personal relationships get destroyed. There is stony ground.

3. Like the *choked plants* (v. 18)? We've been here before. Ten years ago we have a great thing going in our church. We had a scheme to visit house-bound people. We drew up a strategy. We reorganized the pastoral system. We got volunteers. But then the vicar left. And little by little, it nearly all ended. Yet a little does remain! Two people are still actually visiting their house-bound, ten years later! There are two of us who are like the thirty-fold return! (v. 20).

4. Like *the rich soil* (v. 20)? Three of us started a drama-group. It went well. All kinds of people from the community joined in. A social worker and a steel worker. Out of this drama-group a woman came and took over running part of the Sunday School. Others joined the church. One family made up a long-standing rift. The originator said, 'I'm amazed that other things came out of it'. He hadn't catered for hundred-fold returns!

5. Like *the sower*? All that work, and what to show for it? All that effort and expenditure on the seeds! All that knocking on doors, all that planning and hard work, and what are the results? They tell us to be patient, but this is beyond a joke.

Many people nowadays see teaching as Jesus' *real* work. They see him primarily as a teacher who incidentally got involved in other things. And they see the church as a teaching agency which incidentally gets involved in other things. But there isn't much teaching in this Gospel, and when it does come it is so obscure that it needs explanation. Why?

For Mark, Jesus is the bringer of the Kingdom; he gets involved in teaching as part of the programme of the Kingdom. The teaching is not the first work, or the main work. It is needed because of the rest of the programme.

So far in the story, almost every incident has been Jesus responding to someone else's need or claim or complaint or hostility. The stories start with someone else's initiative. The only exceptions are when Jesus makes his first announcement about the Kingdom (1:15), when he starts and adds to the disciple-community (1:16ff; 2:13ff; 3:13ff), and when he goes off alone to pray, and when he gets home. Mark notes also that Jesus preaches, but he gives very few details about the content of this preaching. So the teaching in chapter 4 is virtually Jesus' first public initiative of which there is detailed record. But, coming as it does after so many other events, even this initiative is really more of a response to what has gone before.

This becomes clear when we look at the content of this teaching. After such a long wait to be told about Jesus' actual message, this chapter is at first sight very odd. We might expect a revelation about the nature of eternity, or an account of the new law of God for his people (such as Matthew gives us in his chapters 5 to 7), or a manifesto for the divine revolution (which is Jesus' first message according to Luke, in his chapter 4). In fact what we get from Mark is a mysterious, indeed obscure, parable, followed by an even more obscure short discourse about the need for obscurity. Hardly a promising start for a programme of public education!

Chapter 4 makes sense because it is chapter 4 and not chapter 1. The teaching is brought in at this point to interpret events which have already happened.

The basic message of Chapter 4 is in the series of parables. Most of these are about seeds and plants, because the life-process of plants is so clearly a story of hidden life. And this is the point here. The first three chapters are a whirl of events in which there is much conflict, much opposition. People appear on the scene, something happens to them and they are never heard of again. The story is of success and failure, of loose ends, misunderstandings and confusion. This is the 'real world', the world of experience, the sort of world in which the body of Christ will find itself.

What Jesus offers is not the product of research, but revelation. He makes a statement of what can be known only from the inside, just as only a person who has some sort of inside knowledge can tell you what sort of building is planned for a site where the holes are being dug for the foundations. And Jesus' revelation is that behind all this day-to-day activity there is a hidden process at work. A seed is sown, results do not come immediately but they do come. There are hazards and disturbances, but the fundamental objective is not threatened: the harvest comes according to the farmer's plan. The announcement of the Kingdom will not immediately cause people to accept it. The Kingdom itself, and the announcement of it, are mysterious things which cause different types of response, including the responses of hostility and rejection.

This is exactly what has been happening in the first three chapters. The Kingdom of God is properly called Kingdom, because it has great authority — an authority which at least the powers of evil can recognize: at the same time it is present in weakness, it is a mere seed; and the rest of the Gospel story, with its emphasis on the crucifixion, spells out the vulnerability of the Kingdom. There is the revealing of the mystery to those who receive it; at one stage, this is a secret disclosure. But it is not intended to give the hearers a special select privilege. The intention is that the secret is to be made open and disclosed for all. The Gospel is not intended to form a select in-group, separated from the rest of the human race.

It is not possible to predict exactly where successful growth will happen: seed is scattered all over the place and every type of ground is given a chance (in a small, closely packed territory like Israel it is better to 'waste' seed than to 'waste' land).

SPIN-OFFS

1. What has happened in the experience of members of your group, which you could interpret or explain by means of these parables?

Any disciple-community which starts on the Jesus-action will probably start with a busy programme. It will be alert to human need, it will be interrupted and disturbed, it will run into trouble and opposition. This will be the opening phase; then it will need to lay hold of the resources represented by chapter 4; it will have to realize that the curious hit-and-miss effect of its work is not necessarily due to incompetence or misfortune, but is part of a deeper programme of which God is truly in charge. In the strength of this reflection and reassurance it can engage with the deeper and more complex threatenings of storm and madness which are represented by Mark's next group of stories.

2. What is 'sowing the word' for you?

('Sowing the word' is not just preaching, but doing everything Jesus did in chapters 1–3 — his Movement, and your bits in it and from it.)

3. What are you waiting for?

Are you willing to rest, to listen, to be told that things you never reckoned on, dynamics you never foresaw, are also at work?

8. A Movement in Crisis

MARK 13

What on earth is all this about? Is there anything in this chapter which makes any sense to you?

Up till now, Mark has given us a reasonably straightforward story. But 'abomination of desolation', stars falling out of the sky, 'Let the reader understand' — you must be joking!

Yet, when we stop to think about it, we do have snaps to this nightmare. We are scared; we are in a terrible world; there seems to be no end to violence and horror and destruction. And the worst thing is, we can't trust our own family and our own people any more. And people talk about our times as being 'apocalyptic'. Are there more snaps than we like to think?

Also, we — like Mark — use 'code words' when we describe situations of crisis.

It's as if someone in 1984 said 'Northern Ireland looks like being Britain's Vietnam', or 'We had to avoid a Munich in the Falklands'. 'Vietnam' and 'Munich' are code-words; they make immediate sense to some, and to others are meaningless unless interpreted; and those who understand the code are gradually dying off.

So, what 'code words' of ours 'snap' with the code words of Mark 13?

STUDIES

Chapter 13 is usually reckoned to be the most obscure section of Mark's Gospel. The difficulties are listed and discussed in commentaries, and they are not our main concern here. Some of them are simply due to the fact that Mark was writing for a very specific group of people who would pick up his code-words and would recognize what he was referring to. He could trust that his reader *would* understand when he used a code-word like 'The Desolating Sacrilege' (v. 14); but we are a long way distant from Mark's immediate situation, and we don't know all his code.

But this is not really the biggest problem with this section of Mark's Gospel. The main problem is not with chapter 13 but with chapters 14 and 15. At first sight, they do not seem to present a problem — they are much more straightforward than chapter 13. But stop and ask, what are they *for*? Why does Mark think that his readers need to have such a lot of information about the manner of Jesus' arrest, trials, and death? Chapter 13 supplies the answer.

Whatever the problems of detail in chapter 13, one thing is clear: the people to whom and for whom that chapter (and therefore the whole Gospel) was written were a threatened, victimized, insecure, tempted, confused community who were in trouble because of their discipleship and because of their commitment to the Kingdom. They would *understand* chapter 13, not because they had a good academic education but because it was actually about them. And because they could understand chapter 13, they could then go on and understand the following chapters. The total message of chapters 13–16 is a message of the living Christ to his people in the present moment. The message is: what you are experiencing now (chapter 13), I have already experienced before you (chapters 14 and 15). I have received and met all this concentrated destructiveness which you are now meeting; I have broken its power, and you can meet me in your world (chapter 16).

So, in this obscure chapter 13, we meet Mark's readers more personally than anywhere else in the story. All the rest of the story is past-tense for them. In chapter 13, it is present-tense. They would be able to say, 'We know what this is about — it's about US! We're part of the story!' For Mark's readers, chapter 13 would be one great marvellous and terrifying Snap.

And you, twentieth-century reader, on the receiving end of Mark's work and witness, try to feel yourself alongside those 'Second Christians', those comrades in discipleship for whom Mark wrote, for whom this chapter would 'click' with their immediate reality.

There are several details which indicate this linkage between the chapters.

1. In the story about Jesus there is strong emphasis on his being 'delivered over': the same word is used for the experience of the disciple-community in chapter 13 (10 occurrences of the word in 14 and 15, 3 in chapter 13).

2. Mark's story of Jesus' death is marked out according to 'watches' — intervals of three hours: the same sense of timing is linked to the community's experience in 13:35.

3. Mark tells us of Jesus' attempt to help the community to cope with its ignorance of the detailed plan (13:33). Salvation is not by knowledge but by alertness, not by education but by discipleship. Incarnation means sharing the human condition, and the human condition is not one of omniscience. Christ is willing to be ignorant (13:32): he may even be mistaken as to the details of the future programme (13:30). This does not matter much. In Mark's story, the Christ, the agent of the Kingdom, does not come with a lot of knowledge and argument. W. B. Yeats' last triumphant words say it: 'Man can only embody truth; he cannot know it'.

4. Before his accusers, Christ is silent and isolated. In the face of untruth, he has nothing to say: he does not get into wrangles of defence and interpretation. In the face of truth, he speaks, acknowledging his identity. For this, and this only, he is condemned. This is the model example of 'saying what you are given to say' (13:11). The only word from him after his trial is the enigmatic question in 15:34 — 'My God, my God, why hast thou forsaken me?'

Jesus does not talk *about* an absent God; he does not say, 'God has forsaken me'. He talks *to* this God who has forsaken him. He asks a question, trusting that there is an answer; but he does not know the answer. 'God, I'm speaking to you although you're not here; I don't know why you're not here but I know that you know why you're not here.' Many suffering people will understand this in their guts rather than in their head. But Jesus takes this human ignorance himself; he claims it and makes it part of the programme of the Kingdom. And so, this feeling and this complaint have their proper place in the experience of the disciple-church also: they remain part of incarnation.

In his action at the Last Supper, Jesus connects the truth of his own story to our own discipleship. He takes the bread and says, This is my body: this bread is being broken, as my body is going to be broken. This cup is being poured out, as my blood is going to be shed. This that is happening to these things is happening to me. But it doesn't stop there: I am asking you to understand what I am doing: I am inviting you to participate, to take and eat and drink, to allow yourselves to share in this same programme. This is my way, a new way, of making a covenant, a bond or commitment which is for the human race as a whole and not just for you.

Mark was writing for a suffering and witnessing community. They would have several urgent questions, which he tried to meet.

1. They were a group of people who made no secret of the fact that their leader suffered the fate reserved for convicted terrorists. Crucifixion was, as far as the State was concerned, legitimate counter-revolutionary violence. So, who could blame the Roman authorities if they assumed that the Christian movement was a danger to the State? Mark made a point of showing that Jesus, and therefore Jesus' community, is not guilty of conventional political subversion.

2. Mark also stressed that Jesus was not guilty under the best moral law, the law of the Hebrew Scriptures which the religious authorities claimed as their guide.

3. But there was a deeper and more disturbing question that even those. It could be framed thus:

> If we are right in claiming that Jesus is innocent of both subversion and blasphemy and if we are right in claiming that we also are innocent of these charges, brought by the best legal and religious systems that we know, how is it that Jesus has been crucified and how is it that we also are hammered as we are? The only possible explanation seems to be that there is no justice or truth anywhere any more, and that God is no longer God. It's all very well to be heroic and sacrificial, but is there any point at all?

Part of the answer to this is, of course, in the resurrection. But Mark gives an answer also in the very form in which he writes his story. Spend some time with a text like the RSV which gives Old Testament references. See how they come packed into chapters 14 and 15 like the nerve ends in a sensitive part of the body. Mark is in effect saying, God is not dethroned: the whole of the story, with the exception of a few details of time and place, can be expressed in words drawn from texts which we call God's Word. Strange though it may seem, this is God's plan working out. God knows that this is the kind of world that it is, and he is sharing in it. He is not sending anyone to do a job which he won't touch himself. He is in it, and he reigns. This is the way that things do happen when he takes a place for himself within his creation, and he invites you to join in this happening.

And the story ends where it does, with just the announcement of Resurrection. Resurrection is the end of the past. There is no more story to offer, because from this moment we are in the present and it's all happening now.

SPIN-OFFS

1. Where is the life of our Christian community up to in the sequence of chapters 13 to 16?

2. Where are some brother and sister Christians, in some other part of the world or of the Church, in this passion sequence?

3. Or, Are we nowhere, yet, in the passion sequence because we have not yet got far in Jesus' lifetime sequence (chapters 1–12) — we have not yet got into action for which we could be criticized, much less crucified?

PART THREE

Passages

9. Introduction

In chapter 2, 'How we study the Gospels', we suggested a way of approaching a specific passage. Here we give seven examples of this programme in action.

Most of these examples are taken from Mark's more complex and extended stories. For a group which wants to work its way imaginatively into the Gospel, these have obvious advantages. But we hope that, all in all, we have made a reasonably representative selection from the total Gospel.

Commentators are skilled at classifying stories into various categories. But there really is only one type of story. All the stories, whether they are pronouncement stories or healing stories or whatever, are primarily stories of 'salvation'. They are all signs of the creative presence of God in the world in the person of Jesus. Every story represents the attack of Christ on those forces which threaten to ruin the creation. There is nothing really more 'miraculous' about the healing of the paralytic than there is about the calling of the disciples or the controversies about the Sabbath.

For a discipleship-group, the differences that matter are the differences between the various situations to which Jesus responds. In the presence of one sort of disorder, Jesus says 'Your sins are forgiven'; to another he says 'Come out, unclean spirit'. He doesn't assault the helpless paralytic: equally, he doesn't kindly forgive the oppressive demon. If you find that your Christian discipleship requires you to follow a tricky pattern of reconciliation one day, confrontation the next, you're probably close to Jesus' style of life.

In the following examples, the 'Studies' section is usually the longest. This is only because this is the most objective section, the part that we can best provide from here. In practice, your 'Snaps' section can be quite long, if it enables people really 'to take the material on board'. And the 'Spin-offs' section should never be rushed, because it's at this point that the story starts to have its day-to-day effect in the discipleship of your group.

10. The Paralytic

MARK 2:1–12

Who do you identify with?

I am *the paralysed man*, the patient. I know what it's like to be pushed around on a trolley like a dish of mince. I know what it's like to be carried on a stretcher, with four people bouncing me around, trying to keep in step with each other. I know what it's like to depend entirely on other people's energy and good will: they will give me attention when it's convenient to them; otherwise — I'm on my own. But I can do nothing for myself. I can't even kill myself.

I am in *the congregation*. I want to listen to the sermon. I resent anyone interrupting. I resent the demands of handicapped people; they look horrible and they take up so much space. They should have their own facilities and be satisfied. I am normal. I can stand on my own two feet. I don't see why I should make way for anyone else. I just don't want to be disturbed. But if someone makes a hole in the roof and bits of ceiling start to fall down my neck, then I'll have to give way.

I am *a stretcher-bearer*. I'm not interested in preachers but I am interested in getting any possible help for my friend. I cannot see any point in anything which is all talk and no action. I know a point comes when I run out of ideas; I just have to hand over.

I am *a scribe*. I have an alert ear for a phoney argument. I do believe it's wrong for people to make fancy claims which they can't substantiate.

More people are damaged by lies than by sickness, so it's important to get things right.

I am *Jesus*. I know what it's like to be frustrated, to have my motives suspected all the time by niggling religious people.

I am *the roof*. I get hacked around by all sorts of people who think that I'm just an obstruction to their plans.

I am *Jesus*. It's my home. I invite people in, and before I've had any time to get on with the meeting, someone interrupts and breaks everything open. It's all very well, but who pays for the roof?

If you are reading the story in a group, divide now into five teams, as described on pages 16–17. Each team can ask, 'Who, in the story, is a problem for me?', and 'For whom am I a problem?' Then let the Jesus group ask itself. 'What exactly are we talking about when we speak of "faith"?'

'Jesus saw their faith', it says — faith not of the patient but of the stretcher-bearers. What is 'faith' here? Not an invisible 'spiritual' force but something that can be seen. Not reliance on an outside force, but making the most of one's own energies and initiatives. Not a compensation for one's own feebleness but vigorous, determined, controversial action.

Faith is in the stretcher-bearers: the scribes and Pharisees demonstrate non-faith. They prefer theological debate to costly action. They can only *preserve*; they can't heal.

Faith sees that there are limits. Faith, in this case, does not heal: it brings a person within range of healing. Faith hands over. The man is let down. He can look up at his friends as he descends from them, faces receding, looking down at him around the hole in the roof.

Why does Jesus make this strange first remark? Instead of attending to the need for healing, he says, 'Your sins are forgiven'. This starts an argument about forgiveness. But quite apart from the Pharisees' argument, isn't this an absurd opening comment? How can a man, lying helpless on a stretcher, have sins to forgive? But this is a fundamental claim by Jesus. He insists that the paralytic is in fact still a responsible human being. If the paralytic has no sins to forgive, he is either divine or sub-human. Jesus in effect says, 'You are more than your paralysis, you are not merely a victim. You are a genuine, responsible human being.' If a person can recognize this, and accept the authority of the one who affirms it, the healing of paralysis can follow in its due place.

Mark puts one story within another. When he does this, he shows how Jesus is caught up in a conflict of interest, and this seems to be a common experience for those who seek to be agents of God's kingdom in the world. Jesus is being pulled in various directions, with several different demands being made on him at once; and those who make the demands, or have expectations of him, are at odds with each other.

The effect of healing is that the patient is changed from being a burden to being a carrier. He carries the bed which once carried him. He is able to move freely and responsibly, by his own energy. When people do this, it is a sign that the Kingdom has come near.

Another effect of the healing is that the man is sent home. This is a more important point than it sounds; it is often noted in the healing stories of Jesus. Sickness takes away a person's place within the community. In Jesus' day, the sick were often outcast, homeless, wanderers — most obviously in the case of those suffering from leprosy or madness. When he heals a person, Jesus restores to that person his or her lost rights. In the case of the leper, Jesus sends the healed person to claim his rights from the public health authorities (Mark 1:44). In the case of the paralytic, and of the madman with the 'Legion' (5:19), he restores the healed person to a home community. At this moment, the sending home is a sign of the Kingdom, the rebuilding of a broken community. The crowd recognizes this, and is delighted.

SPIN-OFFS

Who, in the story, is a model for the Church?

Jesus? The Church is the body of Christ. Jesus shows what an event of the Kingdom looks like. The Church is mandated to continue to act out events of the Kingdom, to act as a body to maintain Christ's bodily life. The local church has to work out its policy for acting as a healing and forgiving community. It has to tell people that they can be forgiven; it has to say words of forgiveness; but it also has to act in such a way that people know that the past has no power to hold them. It has to enable people to move freely, to take responsibility for themselves. How does the local church hold together its attention to physical and spiritual disorder? How does it sort out its priorities? What kinds of paralysis are claiming its attention?

The stretcher-bearers? The Church's task is to show people Christ, not to draw attention to its own qualities. Its role is sometimes temporary. It has to let people down and let people go, not enforcing some new kind of dependency. It has to be a genuine community of support, not a group of fussy nuisances who feel compelled to keep themselves in business. The Church needs to work in small teams. Four people may be needed to cope with the needs of one paralytic: they will need to know each other and they will have to walk in step with each other. They may have to abandon the listening congregation in order to care. They may have to do very disturbing things in order to care. Who pays?

The congregation in the house? The Church will probably discover, if it thinks about it, that it is fulfilling this role only too well! It can be so concerned about its own agenda that it cannot make room for the needs of those outside. The 'normal' make the rules and the timetables; they fill the place so that the 'abnormal' can't get in. Those who are vertical don't make room for the horizontal. They pride themselves on being able to stand on their own feet.

The scribes? The other obstructive group. The Church also fulfils this role from time to time. It has to make sure that, in its enthusiasm for orthodoxy and proper standards, it does not get its priorities mixed up and exclude the very people who most need the healing action of Christ.

The patient? The Church is not separated from the sickness and paralysis of the world. The Church is part of the problem as well as being part of God's response. Where is the Church feeling its paralysis? Who carries the helpless Church into the presence of the living Christ?

The praising onlookers? (v. 12) The Church recognizes, and celebrates, the saving act of Christ. It watches for signs of his presence. It knows the stories of Christ's characteristic actions, and it will point them out to the world around. It will take these old stories and see them re-enacted in its contemporary setting.

The house-owner? The Church is almost bound to be the loser, if it is obedient to its Lord. Its property will be knocked around, and it won't be able to give high priority to repairs.

11. Celebrating or Fasting?

MARK 2:18–20

1. Who have you ever seen doing a fast?

2. Have you ever fasted? What was your experience?

3. How is fasting different from slimming?
   (A Christian Aid Factsheet says £253 million was spent on slimming programmes in 1982!)

4. What is the point — if any — of fasting?

The early Church fasted. Jesus assumed people would fast. In Matthew 6:16–18, Jesus says: 'Do not fast so as to be seen by others'. Jesus fasted during the temptation (Luke 4). In Mark 2:20, it is inferred that Jesus' disciples fasted. Colossians 2:16–23 deprecates hypocritical fasting. But churches in Acts 13:2 and 14:23 fasted spontaneously. In 2 Corinthians 6:5 and 11:27, Paul fasted, or at least went hungry.

One possibility is that the early Christians fasted as a secret way of preparing themselves to endure hardship or imprisonment. They needed to be ready to suffer deprivation, if they were arrested. 'Hunger strikes' in prisons are powerful weapons today, and could well have been necessary either when self-imposed or as imposed by authorities, for early Christians.

The time to fast is not to fast when everyone else is fasting, but when it is right for the individual or group. There is no way to lay down rules. Fasting should not be done just because it is a rule or custom or a discipline imposed by some organization. Disciple groups have to do what they feel is right for them.

The fasting is really irrelevant. Whether it is fasting or feasting is not really the point. The point is that there is a new leader — the Bridegroom. And this new leader, Jesus, is the replacement for both John the Baptist and the Pharisees. Disciples simply have to do what the leader does. The question for disciples is always, 'What is the leader doing? Is he celebrating or is he fasting?' Or, 'With whom is he celebrating, and with whom is he fasting?' Or, 'What do we need to do now, fast or celebrate, to put his mission into visible form?'

With whom is Jesus celebrating? Jesus has just stated, 'I came not to call the righteous, but sinners'. So it is clear that sinners are those with whom he is celebrating. The righteous are fasting. To fast means not just to go hungry; it means to share in a community's abstention from celebration. The righteous are already in a community, either the community of the Pharisees or the community of John. They are already in a feast, so fasting is a proper option for them. Up till now, the sinners have not been able to fast; they have had no choices; all they could do was to go hungry. They have not been in any community which could celebrate, so they could not abstain from celebrating either. But Jesus says, 'I am calling sinners'. I am giving sinners also a chance to share in a community of celebration. I am restoring to them a place at table. The banquet is open to them, a banquet which up to now has been a no-go area for them. So they are in a celebration. The wedding is happening. When the wedding ceremony is over, when the new community is made, then they will also be able to fast. They will be in a community which can choose whether to feast or fast.

We fast as members of a community which can celebrate with Jesus — not just as individual slimmers! How does it happen? What, in practice, is the fasting? Is it merely a reversal of celebration? Is it beating your breast, putting ashes on your head? Or is it a certain number of ounces to eat for each meal — 1, 2 and 5 ounces?

In July 1978 a group of members of the Eucharist Congregation in Sheffield decided to fast once a week. This arose over a period of awareness that they needed some disciplined and demanding way of expressing their concern over world hunger and over-affluence. Up to a dozen people for two years maintained this weekly fast, meeting occasionally to support each other in it, and to decide what to do with the money of the 'Fast Fund' (a jam-jar received each Eucharist the cost of meals saved).

For many of the group, fasting has become a form of celebration rather than deprivation, an action of hope rather than despair, a way of escape from the domination of our stomachs. One member has put it, 'Fasting is a high point in the week. It liberates me, I feel more in control. When I eat again, I appreciate the food much more intensely, but also feel a sort of let-down, a return to normal from a special time — which is a celebration of myself vis-à-vis the world.'

SPIN-OFFS

1. What are the reasons for fasting today?

2. Do you need to fast in order to celebrate? Celebrate your liberation from over-eating and indulgence? The Eucharist Congregation in Sheffield said:

When we fast, we do it as a kind of celebration.

It is not a hopeless thing, but it is a hope for the future.

We feel good about, we enjoy it.

Just the fact that we can fast is a good thing and gives us a good feeling.

3. There are biological results from fasting, such as that I am just not able to eat as much as I did before. I thus prepare myself biologically for any coming world-scarcity of food.

4. Fasting and celebrating also have visibility. Everyone now knows about Moslem discipline, because of Ramadan fasts, dawn to sunset. How should Christians be 'visible'? What about Jesus' 'fast secretly'? Does it mean:

'Net curtains at t'window
And nowt on t'table'?

That is, keeping a show of prosperity when there is poverty within?

12.   The Gadarene Swine

MARK 5:1–20

I am the patient. I'm on my own, outside society. No one wants me. I am no use. They try to tie me up; I can break my chains, but I'm not free. I've got no control over myself. I'm occupied; there's someone else who keeps on speaking on my behalf.

I am the patient, healed. I'm alright now; but still no one around wants me. No one seems happy about it. I think they would all prefer me to be ill — they would have something to complain about. I would like to leave this place and go along with the man who has straightened me out. But he says 'No — You've a job to do at home'.

I am a pig-keeper. We've lost our jobs. Big herds are a thing of the past now.

I am the pig-owner — and the general public. Is one man's sanity worth 2,000 pigs? Jesus out!

I am the demons. We have made a nice little colony here. We are secure. It's far better than home. We have real authority. We can tell this man who he is and can speak up on his behalf.

STUDIES

For Mark, the world of demons was not an occult, distant world: it was very much part of a contemporary, real world. People felt that they were in hell, that hell was very close. Heaven and hell were not states far away on the far side of death. And Christ fundamentally reduces the power of death so that it no longer acts as a boundary. He brings heaven to earth; and he also forces the powers of hell into disclosing themselves. Christ discloses and overcomes the alienation in the world, the sin of the world.

This demon-possessed man is one who is fundamentally alienated, alienated from his own will, his own speech, his own self. His mind is populated with images of destruction and terror.

For the people of the New Testament, there were two kinds of sickness. There was functional disorder, which might be a physical or sensory disability like deafness or paralysis; and there was fundamental disorder, which meant that the whole being was in some way inhuman. This latter was thought of as demon-possession.

Demons were irrational, and their choice of victims was not a punishment for anything. Demon-possession was not a sign of guilt. So it was possible to make a clear distinction between the demon and the demon's victim. Jesus attacks the demon with aggression and competence (he destroys the enemy by using the enemy's own strength — the Christian Judo technique?), and he supports the demon's victim with compassion and hope.

This distinction is very necessary when we are conscious of people being possessed by massive corporate demons such as racial prejudice. It does no good to blame people for attitudes derived from nurturing and environment: equally it does no good to tolerate the presence of a destructive spiritual force. A *person* can be forgiven: a *demon* has to be destroyed. To say to a demon 'your sins are forgiven' is to tolerate disorder, to placate evil, and to refuse assistance to the oppressed and the exploited.

This story is set in a border-land. Here, there is a huge herd of unclean animals which would not be allowed in the religious heart-land of Judaism. Here, there is a cliff full of little caves, a burial place, a place of uncleanness and the power of death. Here, there is a man of this half-caste area, fragmented in himself, breaking himself up, driving himself to destruction. He rejects and defeats all those who want to control him. He keeps up a violent monologue with himself. Everything about him is valueless. This is his story and his song.

The man acknowledges Jesus' authority. He takes the initiative. As at Mark 1:24, the power of evil recognizes holiness more quickly than does established religion. But when Jesus commands, the demon resists the authority it has recognized. Jesus orders the demon out, but the demon wishes to stay put. Notice in verses 6 to 11, how Mark gets confused between the patient and the demons, between 'he' and 'they'. The demons answer on behalf of the man. The man has no name, no voice, no identity and no will of his own. He is taken over. He has only the name of the demon, and the demon gives itself the name 'Legion', the name of a unit of the Roman army, the army which was at that moment occupying and controlling the area. Mark carefully puts this Latin word into Greek. Thousands of alien forces have taken up habitation; they have turned the place into a colony, and they claim the right to speak on behalf of the native population. They like it there: they don't want to go home. If they have to leave, they will want to go to some other place where they can continue to exploit the local area. But they must not just be let loose. Colonists are damaging, dangerous beings; their powers of destruction have to be discharged. So they are sent off to the 2,000 pigs, and the full force of their destructiveness is seen.

If you are working on this story in a group, divide now into four teams: one for the man, one for Jesus, one for the pig-keepers and pig-owners, one for the general public. Ask the questions: 'Is one man's sanity worth 2,000 pigs?' and 'What do you think should be done about this situation?'

The cost is colossal: is it worth it? This story shows that although Jesus has remarkable powers he doesn't put things right by magic or by almighty exercises of will. There is a cost to be paid in the struggle: evil doesn't just go away by people thinking nice thoughts. The pigs have a cash value; they create employment. Is therefore the sanity of one man worth 2,000 pigs? The general public says No. Jesus is asked to leave. He goes.

Until the insane man met Jesus, he was outcast.

For his restoration, the demons have to be outcast.

To ensure that their destructiveness is contained with minimum danger, the pigs have to be outcast.

To prevent any more disturbances to the neighbourhood, Jesus is outcast.

The insane man's worthlessness comes to rest on Christ. He bears the cost, the ostracism. He bears the disorder himself. He takes away the sin of the world.

The healed person asks to be allowed to join the disciple-group. In some other cases (e.g. 10:52), Jesus allows this. Here he says, 'I'm going away; I've got a job for you here'. Normally, Jesus insists that there should be no publicity for his work of healing; here, he gives the healed man a responsibility for publicity. Jesus doesn't want him as a dependent 'adherent'; he wants him as an evangelist. The man is to go and tell people about the work and the mercy of the Lord. He is to go into a diseased society as evidence of a new state of things. The story has already been told in the area, and the people haven't liked it at all; he is to go and tell the story again. He is to evangelize in that most difficult of all environments, home.

SPIN-OFFS

1. How do we diagnose what is wrong in our area?

2. What really is the cost of healing?

3. What loss is caused to the community when people are made whole?

4. What sort of approval should a healing Church expect?

5. What demons have taken hold of which of us?

13. Jairus and the Woman

MARK 5:21–43

An African woman said: 'To me, the two stories are the contrast between healing at home and healing in hospital. At home, it can all be in private; but hospital forces personal details into the open.'

I am Jairus. I am a powerful person, but I'm prepared to descend to recognizing unorthodox and unrespectable people to get what I desperately want in emergency.

I am the woman, anonymous and unknown. I have had no energy for years. No way of making my presence felt or my needs known. I'm drained. I'm empty of blood and empty of money.

I am Jesus. My life is a series of interruptions. I'm not allowed to get on with my programme of work, even when it's most urgent.

I am Jairus. I'm supposed to be the big man around here, but at the moment of this matter of life and death along comes someone with a quite unimportant matter which could easily wait till tomorrow.

I am a professional mourner. I go around helping people to make a good demonstration of woe and sorrow. I help to create an atmosphere of gloom and mourning to ease people's pain. If death is not allowed to have its way, I'll be out of a job.

I am the daughter. I don't really know what is happening. No one has asked my opinion about any part of all this. But I'm glad that someone realizes that all this excitement can make one hungry.

STUDIES

This is another example of Mark's technique of offering a story within a story. There is a powerful set of contrasts between the two patients.

Ask, in small teams, what is the problem faced by Jesus? What is the problem faced by the woman? What is the problem faced by Jairus?

Start with the inner story. The woman is in a continual and chronic state of haemorrhage, a constant menstruation. According to Jewish law and tradition, any woman was unclean and outside the community of holiness during her monthly period; this woman is excluded from the community of holiness not just for about 40 days a year but for 365. She has to be excluded, as part of the scheme by which the respectable citizens of the religious system can be kept respectable. Her excludedness is the price paid for the people's purity. And whose job is it to ensure that she is excluded? Whose task is it, to ensure that the rules of religion are properly obeyed? Who other than Jairus, the ruler of the synagogue? In their roles, Jairus and the woman are enemies; their interests are fundamentally incompatible. We could express the contrast in tabular form:

CONTRASTS AND COMPARISONS
BETWEEN THE TWO PARTS OF THE STORY

Jairus	The Woman
He is in authority in the religious system.	She is a victim of the religious system.
He is a person of privilege in the culture.	She is rejected by the culture.
He is named.	She is anonymous.
He is socially secure.	She is socially excluded.
He is male, father, surrounded by family.	She is female, isolated, with no support.
He is able to request attention.	She is voiceless, has to grab attention.
He claims on behalf of another.	She has no one to claim on her behalf.
He sacrifices his public dignity.	She loses her secrecy and privacy.
He is a public person, makes a public request, gets healing in private.	She is a private person, makes secretive approach, gets healing in public.

Jairus	The Woman
He asks Jesus to touch the patient.	She touches without asking.
He falls before Jesus, before healing.	She falls before Jesus, after healing.
His professional duty is to operate the regulations concerning uncleanness.	She has, for a long time, been a victim of regulations concerning uncleanness.
Custom and law tell him that he has the right to approach.	Custom and law tell her that she must keep away.
He searches for Jesus.	Jesus searches for her.

THE TWO PATIENTS

The daughter of Jairus	The Woman
She is the hope for her family's future.	She has no future, only a miserable past.
She is 12 years old.	She has been losing life-blood for 12 years.
She represents the future hope for the nation (of 12 tribes).	She represents the past tragedy of the nation (of 12 tribes).
She is in very acute emergency.	Her condition is chronic; today is no different to any previous day.
She is at age of starting to be menstrual, her physical system coming to completeness.	She is continuously menstrual, her physical system all deranged.
Her life is being wasted.	Her financial livelihood has been wasted.
Her situation is beyond normal human help.	Her situation is beyond medical help.
Her healing happens when she is the centre of attention.	Her healing happens when everyone is concerned about someone else.
Jesus reduces the public attention around her.	Jesus increases the attention around her.
Jairus refers to her as his daughter.	Jesus addresses her as 'Daughter'.
She, the daughter of privilege, has to wait for Jesus' attention.	She, the outsider, interrupts, and Jesus attends to her first.
Jairus asks for her to be 'saved' and to be given 'life'.	Jesus tells her that she has been 'saved'.
Word of healing: 'Arise' — be resurrected.	Word affirming healing: 'Your faith has saved you.'
She, the daughter of privilege, is restored to a place in the sharing of food in the household.	She, the outsider, is restored to a place in the '*shalom*', the peace and justice of God.

'FAITH' IN THE TWO PARTS OF THE STORY

Jairus	The Woman
Jesus demands that Jairus must have faith.	Jesus recognizes that she has faith.
Faith is expressed in making a request.	Faith is expressed in grasping.
Faith is refusal to be discouraged by the fact of death.	Faith is refusal to be discouraged by religious rules.
Faith means being willing to disregard a stated fact and a public message.	Faith means being willing to disregard a very deep public attitude.

THE EXPERIENCE OF JESUS
IN THE TWO PARTS OF THE STORY

In the 'Jairus' part	In the 'Woman' part
Jesus perceives a word which he is not supposed to hear.	Jesus perceives a touch which he is not supposed to feel.
People laugh at Jesus.	People protest at Jesus.
Jesus brings the disciples in to see.	The disciples fail to see.
Jesus has a 'prestige' patient.	Jesus is interrupted by an 'inferior' patient.
Jesus insists on being a bringer of hope, in spite of being ritually contaminated.	Jesus finds himself to be ritually contaminated by the woman, and strongly commends her for her action.
Jesus brings a new life, which is not just a continuation of the old.	Jesus brings a new life, in which the old laws of exclusion have no more authority.
Jesus brings 'salvation' to the child of the privileged, a salvation which has first been gained by the unprivileged.	Jesus allows himself to be delayed by the apparently non-urgent needs of the unprivileged.

The two patients need each other to point up their two situations. The woman has been in her condition, excluded, disinherited, for all the years during which Jairus' daughter has been growing up to be a nice acceptable member of the society of the inheritors.

Jairus is so obviously the person in extreme need. Everyone will sympathize with him. And yet, during these last precious minutes while his daughter's life hangs in the balance, while all the ambulance sirens are wailing madly, he has to cope with this unreasonable delay, caused by a woman who could so easily hang on another few hours.

Why does Jesus allow himself to be diverted? Because in his eyes the woman's condition is not less urgent than the condition of the little girl.

If he had not allowed himself to be diverted, the woman would not have been brought out into the open: she would not have been required to put herself into words; she would not have come to realize that her unlawful, surreptitious adventure of touching Jesus' clothes was in fact just the sort of defiance of convention that Jesus needed to enable healing to take place; she would not have heard that her action, which she rightly thought would be condemned by religious opinion, in fact won Jesus' praise. And if she had not been thus brought out into the public, we would not have been able to hear of this definition of faith; and if we had not been given this clear evidence of Jesus' approval of her action, we would not have the mandate to destroy the whole mythology of uncleanness which the woman represents. Jesus has to have time to announce his pleasure and commendation at her unlawful action: by so doing, he knocks away a taboo which still has its lingering power where religion is dominated by a male world-view.

So, it was essential for Jesus to allow himself to be interrupted and delayed. But the crisis of Jairus' daughter's approaching death is not slowed down during the delay. She reached the crisis and passes it. There is no nick-of-time rescue. The one who is secure in religious identity is allowed to die while priority is given to the one who is insecure. Only on the far side of death is there new life and hope for the secure. And Jairus has to allow his daughter to be attended by a man who has been contaminated by contact with someone whom he, Jairus, is supposed to keep out.

Faith is necessary for both healings. Faith is there, unbidden, in the insecure, rejected woman. Faith has to be bidden and encouraged in the privileged man. And the faith which is required of him is much the same as the faith commended in the woman — a faith to accept that the woman's contact with Jesus does not disqualify him from being a source of the healing power of God. To the woman, Jesus says, 'Your faith has saved you' — and the verb has the combined meanings of saving and healing. He does not claim that he has healed and saved: your salvation is your own responsibility. Jesus does not go round drawing attention to his success. He is not greedy for miracles. He is not trying to prove anything. He does not earn a living this way. He wants no publicity. But he is the bringer of the Kingdom. Where he is, healing happens. He is in the world where people are, with a hem of garment that people can touch.

For Mark and his readers, this complex story would have been very close to home. How can it be right, Jewish Christians must have said, for outsiders who have been in the darkness for centuries to be treated as so urgent while the pressing needs of Jews seem to be ignored? And the answer came that those who are inside are continually having their situation reshaped by those who are outside. The daughter of Judaism had to die, and had to be raised into a Church deeply modified by the Gentile mission.

SPIN-OFFS

1. For the 'insiders'

We hear the same anxieties within the contemporary Church. Where are the priorities? With those who have been in the Church for generations or with those who by one means or another have been kept out? And the same problems apply to the clashes of interest between rich and poor, old and young, workers and unemployed, host community and immigrants. The answer is that those who are inside get divine attention which has been given first to those who are outside.

2. For the despairing

Those who are inside will come to the point of saying, There's no use bothering now, we lost our chance, God has no time for us, there's no future for us, the bearer of fertility for new generations is dead. There is no new womb coming along, no one new to bleed in preparation for new life, no new source of milk and caresses to renew a springtime for our people. Our twelve-year-old girl is dead and all we can hope for is to grow old and see the place taken over by strangers.

But Christ says, Don't weep; and don't mock, either. Believe the strange timing of a God who is master of his delays, whose priorities are not perverse, who is not merely trying to curb the impatience of the privileged. Have faith in one who overcomes the divide, who brings the privileged and the unprivileged into a common fellowship of the healed, with the unprivileged leading the way. Have faith in one who will come to attend you when he has been contaminated by contact with someone whom you could not attend. The daughter of religion has to die, and is raised into a new world of salvation where the healed alien is there before her.

3. For the impatient

The Church, locally and nationally, may be longing for new life, yearning, acting and searching for it. But there may have to be delay before we can hear the call to us 'Child, arise', before we can eat in the new hope. Maybe we have to wait, because first of all there is someone else waiting, someone bleeding outside, waiting for a hem of a garment to be available to touch.

14. The Desert Meal

MARK 6:30–44

1. Snaps with the Crowd

Five thousand is a lot of people!

A desert place is a terrifying prospect!

Have you ever been in a situation like this? A football crowd that goes mad? A crowded train in a crash? A mob that follows its worst elements?

The clue is that a crowd develops its own life — its own internal dynamic. But, equally, its dynamic arises out of the life and issues of its time.

2. Snaps with the Feeding

Have you ever been at an occasion anything like this? Feeding thousands of starving refugees? Or a mass open-air celebration at which the Eucharist is shared?

Or is your church's communion service in any way a 'snap' with this story?

STUDIES

There seem to be two dominant motifs running through the story of the Desert Meal.

1. It sounds like a Holy Meal, a Eucharist.

There are many parallels between 6:30–46 and 8:1–26. Indeed, even the other stories before and after look similar. This can be indicated in the following way:

Five Thousand	Four Thousand
Many people 6:33	Large crowd 8:1
Meal 6:34–46	Meal 8:1–10
Storm 6:47–52	—
Debates with Pharisees 7:5–23	Debates with Pharisees 8:11–21
Syrophoenician woman 7:25–30	—
Deaf mute 7:32–37	Blind man 8:22–26

All this makes clear that the feeding stories are to be seen as related to other conflict stories — storms, debates, dramatic healings.

But, beyond this, there are other parallels which suggest that the meals are to be thought of as in a special way related to the meal that the Christians observed to obey Jesus' command at the Last Supper. There is a striking way in which the various elements follow each other:

Five Thousand 6:41–43	Four Thousand 8:6–8	The Last Supper 14:22–23
taking the five loaves and two fish	He took the seven loaves	As they were eating he took bread
he looked up to heaven and blessed	and having given thanks	and blessed
and broke the loaves	he broke them	and broke it
and gave them to the disciples	and gave them to the disciples	and gave it to them.
to set before the people.	to set before the people.	

And he taking the fish	They had a few small fish and having blessed them he commanded that these	And he took a cup and when had given thanks
divided it among them.	should be set before them	he gave it to them
And they all ate	And they ate	and they all drank of it.
and were satisfied.	and were satisfied.	

So, we have to see this feeding story as part of the whole tradition about Jesus 'taking, blessing, breaking and giving'. The Last Supper was important because it was the 'last' time the earthly Jesus did this. And he ended that occasion by asking them to carry on doing it — to carry on taking and sharing, as they had done in the desert meal.

Now, we turn to the second dominant motif in the passage.

What do you think the Roman government would make of the story? Does it not sound like a mob getting ready to revolt? At least, we can say:

2. It sounds like a threatening crowd.

Five thousand men at one sitting is quite a crowd. Matthew adds that there were women and children as well (Matthew 14:21)! What were they doing there? John's Gospel says that they had come to make Jesus their King (John 6:15), and this might well be a clue to the whole episode.

It is hard to put ourselves into the position of people living in an enemy-occupied country, such as Palestine was in Jesus' day.

Alan T. Dale once told us a remarkable story of his own experience which helped him understand this better. He wrote:

'In 1929 I went out to China and in 1933 the Japanese invasion of Manchurea, North China, took place. They came as far south as Tientsin, occupying Callhope, although they publicly denied their military presence there. This was in the "Demilitarized Zone" south of the Manchurian border. They occupied T'angshan, the railway and mining town which was the centre of our Christian work in the north (in Hepei), with Fred Heslop in charge. I was in Shantung, and had to go north to T'angshan to see Fred, who was ill. So I had several times to move in and out of the area occupied by Japanese troops.

'So for the first time I lived in an "occupied country", and saw the effect this had on the life and attitudes and conversation of ordinary Chinese people. Suddenly, I found myself realizing that this was the situation in which Jesus grew up, and in which he carried out his ministry. The conversation with every meal in which he shared must have been very like the conversations I listened to. There, whatever the subject, the Japanese presence forced itself into the talk.

'I began to read Mark's story of Jesus in quite a different way. What Jesus had to say — his stories and remarks and sayings — took on a new liveliness and "bite". This impression and awareness deepened when I re-read Flavius Josephus' *Jewish War*, and years later, read the Israeli account of the freedom fighters, the Zealots, given in such books as Yigael Yadin's *Masada*.

'The desert meal with a group of 5,000 men looks to me like a mob looking for a way to become an effective resistance movement. The tragedy of the great Resistance movement up to the capitulation at Masada was that it had no *leader*. There was a whole succession of Messianic and Zealot leaders — but no one of them could gain total support. So, here, five thousand look to Jesus as the Leader in a revolt against the Romans.'

So wrote Alan Dale. What evidence is there for this? Well, there are some remarkable elements in the story itself.

1. The crowd itself. Mark's word 'men' means men as distinct from women or children. Matthew says it was 5,000 men, without (in Greek, *choris*) women and children (14:21).

2. The division into 50's and 100's invites comparison with the divisions of Roman legionaries into 50's and 100's, or of the Jews in the wilderness (Exodus 18:21).

3. The reference to sheep without a shepherd in Old Testament usage 'regularly means an army without a general, a nation without a national leader' (T. W. Manson). The Shepherd in passages like 1 Kings 22:17, Micah 5:5f, etc., exercises political, religious and military leadership.

4. 'Many were coming and going' (v. 31) could refer to people engaged in preparations for a Messianic uprising.

5. The crowd reaching the rendezvous ahead of Jesus and the disciples (v. 33) suggests a premeditated scene.

6. The 'many things' taught by Jesus (v. 34b) could be his long explanation of why he could not be the leader they hoped for.

7. Jesus departing afterwards to pray (v. 46) suggests that Jesus needed help after a unique ordeal.

Jesus, we must remember, grew up in a country in which revolt and insurgence were common experiences. Japhia, a walled town two miles from Nazareth, was a centre of resistance movements. The Tenth Legion reduced it to rubble in AD 67. Josephus says it sided with the Maccabees in 168 BC. Judas of Galilee and his sons and grandsons led the resistance, and much of Galilee supported them. 'Bandit' was a technical word for 'resister'. It was impossible for Jesus not to have been related in some way to the Resistance. Later, opponents of Paul were resistance movement followers, attempting to lynch him.

So, we have a highly political scene, and a meal. The meal was thus 'political'. It was a dramatic meal, a disciplined and symbolic way of sharing food. There are many other examples of food being used in this sort of way. For instance, at Masada in AD 73, Jewish resisters shared their resources together before finally committing suicide together. But if we take just this one example of Masada, and compare it with the meal which Jesus leads, we can see some of the special features of Jesus' meal which are permanently important for us.

Masada meal	**Jesus' meal**
The last celebration of an old movement.	One of the first big gatherings of our new movement.
The final failure of a vision of preservation.	A transformation and a new opportunity which only Jesus brings.
A defiant wastage.	A gathering-up, to avoid waste.
A community that saves itself by being separate from the rabble, from sinners, from collaborators.	A community which gathers together sinners, the lost, the sheep without a shepherd, even collaborators (tax-collectors, etc.).
The desert as a place for withdrawing and dying.	The desert as a place for gathering, nourishing, assembling, training.
Table-fellowship for those who are *in*.	Table-fellowship restored to those outside.
Meal to say good-bye to the world and to each other.	Meal seen as public challenge to the authorities of the world.
Meal which challenges the world as a sign of the sacrifice of a tough, clearly-defined community which is shaped by the loyalties of the past.	Meal which challenges the world as a sign of something completely new, a very non-homogeneous community shaped only by the call of Jesus and a vision of the Kingdom which is coming.

The items in the right-hand column above, not the left, are the guiding models of our Eucharistic fellowship. It is the banquet of the Messiah, the Christ-worship which displaces the worship of Caesar. So it is bound to be political; it cannot be just a private hobby. Very soon after these events in the Gospel-story, people gathered for the Eucharist, treasuring these stories; and they quickly became targets for intimidation and repression by the security-systems of the day.

This is how the story can work for Christian disciples in the Church. In the actual experience of Jesus as Mark describes it, this incident was one of Jesus' last attempts to get the people in his Way. Jesus failed. From now on, all the people do not follow him, only 'the crowd', 'those with him' and his disciples. They wanted him as Leader. But he has to lead in his own way, in his own direction, with his own revolution.

SPIN-OFFS

1. We separate Eucharist and revolution. But Jesus rejected one kind of revolution and made another — and Jesus kept Eucharist at the centre of it. 'Taking, and sharing' was part of the Eucharist and part of the revolution. What would it mean to celebrate Eucharist as if it were revolution? And to build a revolution on the model of Eucharist? Draw up some plans for action.

2. Jesus was a man's man, and could have been a great leader. He didn't fight shy of being accepted in terms people could use. Are we too choosy? Do we fear Christianity as a movement? Is the popular acclaim always wrong? Don't we have to lose too many friends to get a following that would really go for revolution?

3. What threat is the Eucharistic congregation of which you are a member? To whom is it a threat?

15. Ephphatha

MARK 7:31–37

I can't hear. I assume everyone else is talking about me.

I can't hear. Unless someone definitely makes it clear that I am being talked to, I assume everyone is leaving me out.

I can't hear. As far as most other people are concerned, for most of the time I needn't exist.

I can't hear. I judge by the way people look, the things they do, the way they touch, not by what they say.

Get the distinction clear between a *disability* and a *handicap*. The *disability* is the malfunction of muscle, eye or ear; it is a fact of life, it can be measured. The *handicap* is what the patient and society make of the disability. Whether the disability constitutes a handicap is largely a matter of other people's attitudes to the disabled person.

There was an Old Testament vision which looked forward to a day when handicaps would be no more, not by the removing of the disabled but by the overcoming of the disability (Isaiah 35:5–7). The blind will see and the deaf hear and the lame leap: they will be part of the community of celebration. This will be on the day of God's vengeance, when God comes to rectify the injustices of society.

This is background to the story of Jesus healing the deaf. Whatever the reasons for the strange journey described in chapters 7–8 (if taken literally on the map it is a real dog's hind leg of a trip), one thing is very clear: every place mentioned is on the frontier, far away from the respectable community of holiness. Isaiah's prophecy tells of the new status that will come to the disabled people and also to the despised and useless places. This is all part of God's 'vengeance'.

Mark uses a very strange Greek word to describe the patient in the story, '*mogilalos*' — stammerer. This may well be a matter of technical accuracy on Mark's part. The man was not strictly 'dumb': deaf people very rarely are. Dumbness, in the sense of a disability of the speech organs, is a rare disorder anyway, and has got no connection with deafness.

Hearing people still sometimes refer to the deaf as 'deaf and dumb', but this is a very ignorant and misleading phrase. The reason why deaf people often speak differently to hearing people is that they haven't been able to learn to speak by hearing. So their speech sounds 'abnormal', and 'stammering' is as good a word as any to describe it. But Mark does not often use rare obscure terms — he is usually a very simple writer. There is only one other place in the whole Bible in Greek where this word is found — Isaiah 35:5. Mark is saying, therefore, that in Jesus this vision is being fulfilled. Jesus has brought this 'day of vengeance'. The future has become present: the handicaps are being dissolved, the barriers are being knocked away, out there in the borderlands.

Here is a group of people who realize that a new possibility is present: they bring the man to Jesus. And Jesus deals with the man with remarkable precision. He does what few hearing people do: he communicates with the deaf in the deaf person's own terms.

So, take the story step by step, and pick out exactly how Jesus communicates.

1. Jesus isolates the patient — not his normal practice, but essential with deaf people. If you don't make it specifically clear that you are trying to communicate with the deaf, the deaf will think that the message is for someone else: they are constantly onlookers at other people's conversation. Jesus accepts, as a starting-point, the fact that this is a man who has been closed off from communication.

2. Jesus uses the communication-methods which come most naturally to the deaf— touch and gesture. This is sign-language, crude and direct. He tells the man what he is intending to do.

3. Jesus uses very precise sign-language, not just the generalized 'laying-on-of-hands' requested. He draws the man into a conspiracy of healing, he helps the man to participate. He doesn't merely 'work a miracle'; he communicates. This is not just 'spiritual' healing; it is sacramental, incarnational, touching the flesh and using the sensory system as far as it will go.

4. So far, there is no speech between Jesus and the deaf man. But Jesus needs to use speech, that most subtle and precise of the media. And Mark records his word, precisely. For the most part, we don't know the words of Jesus; we know his Aramaic speech only through the filters and distortions involved in the process of translation into Greek. But occasionally we hear the actual sounds that he made. And because Mark gives us this original word we can see the extraordinary precision of the word which Jesus used: *'Ephphatha'* is an absolute gift to the lip-reader.

The corresponding word in Greek (*dianoikthēti*) is reasonably possible to lip-read. The translation in a number of other languages is also not too bad. The translation into English is almost impossible — 'be opened' is practically impossible to lip-read clearly. Jesus evidently had the instinct to choose this particular word as a combination of the sense he wished to convey and the method of conveying it to a person with a particular need.

The word is not merely a mouthing; it has a precise meaning. It is an attack on the man's closedness. So the man hears: because he is able to hear, his speech becomes clear. And people realize that in Jesus the new age has come; he is doing things well; he is bringing a new creation, and we can look at what he does and proclaim that it is good.

SPIN-OFFS

What spin-offs in actions and attitudes result from these 'snaps' with the story?

1. The Church is the community of caring: it brings people to Jesus.

2. The Church is the Body of Christ: it works as Jesus worked. It communicates to people in their terms; it learns their language and uses that language to disturb and to heal. The large Church can enable a person to remain closed. The person who needs individual attention may never receive it.

3. The Church is the world, hoping and waiting for change. The deaf Church is the target of the divine opening treatment — patient, appropriate, rigorous.

4. The Church is the praising crowd, observing, recognizing and celebrating God's justice and creative act.

16. Lordship and Discipleship

MARK 8:27–9:1

Try 'snapping' with Jesus. And with Peter. And with the other disciples.

A group of ministers sat around studying this passage. They were trying to recognize Christ and then get in on his action. But they ended up finding that they were more with Peter than with Jesus. They were more inclined to reject the self-denying, suffering role than to share it. They had known rejections (v. 32) and didn't like it.

'Why can't we have Jesus acting as Messiah?' one of them asked. 'Is it really Satanic to want to see the Messiah doing his thing on earth? Is it really of the devil to want to be on the side of a successful Lord? And is it always disloyalty when we get the taste of success and like it?'

One after another they confessed:

> 'We don't understand and we're afraid to ask . . .'

> 'Why the hell did I get mixed up with this character in the first place?'

> 'If I had read Mark first, I'd never have gone into the Church.'

> 'I don't tell anyone, even myself, for I am afraid.'

If you are working in a group, get teams to represent Jesus, Peter, and the other disciples. How do they feel in this story?

STUDIES

The meaning of 8:34–35 is really this:

> If you want to help me, you must give all your heart to it. You must put yourself last. You must be ready to let people do their worst to you. And you must keep your eyes on me. . .
> If you are always thinking of saving your skins, that's just what you won't do. But, if you forget all about yourself because you are keen on helping me, even if you lose your life, you will be all right. You will really be yourself. (*New World*, pp. 118f)

The actual phrase 'Take up the cross and follow me' would have had startling and terrifying implications for Jesus' hearers.

This phrase might have been used by the Zealot movement as a recruiting slogan. The Zealots were the urban guerillas, freedom fighters, terrorists of that day, a nationalist band wholly opposed to the rule of Rome. People were used to the prospect of crucifixion. The confused insurrections which erupted on the death of Herod the Great in 4 BC were eventually crushed by Varus, the Roman general. He crucified 2,000 people to signify the end of the rebellion. The phrase must have hit Jesus' contemporaries with a chill, certainly. Maybe they had seen those 2,000 bodies when they were younger. They would certainly have seen many crucified corpses with the smell of rotting flesh and excrement on the legs. (One of the effects of crucifixion was the release of the bowel's muscle-control.) So, 'take up your cross' was not a reference to mental, psychological or spiritual difficulties, but to bodily annihilation and the negation of bodily functions.

It also had real political implications. Anyone who was crucified was a danger to the State. Perhaps it is not possible for anyone in England really to feel the impact of this phrase. Maybe some who were in the war might get a glimpse. Maybe some who were involved in the paramilitary groups in Ireland could get a good idea. The search for a parallel contemporary phrase is hard. 'To the firing squad' (a cleaner form of death) is close to the meaning, but it is far from our experience.

People on the way to their own execution carried their own cross-beam on which they would be hung. Therefore, to be invited to take up a cross is to be invited to assist in one's own execution. Being a follower of Jesus is to engage in suicide, like the Japanese *kamikaze* pilots during the

1939–45 war — sworn to throw themselves away in their aircraft and so blow up enemy warships — or like the IRA prisoners in the 1980s, committing suicide by hunger-strike.

Is it a hopeless cause? Or, does it just appear from outside to be a hopeless cause? It is certainly an invitation to a cause which will disrupt or destroy the established order. It looks dangerously revolutionary.

Jesus is inviting followers to an apparently lost cause, by following which they will be 'safe'. There will be no apparent success, praise or ultimate (in worldly terms) salvation. Jesus invites people to surrender, to non-conformity, to loss, to destruction.

SPIN-OFFS

1. Cross-Bearing

The 'suburban' image of the Christian looks out of place. So often, Christianity comes across as the image of the 'good' person, the respectable, law-abiding, even self-righteous human being. Christianity appears as the law-and-order religion. It conforms to middle-class standards of behaviour and aims. It fits in well with our notions of success, a place at university or in management. Christianity survives as the do-gooder religion, as time allows after other commitments (family, work, leisure, friends) have been met.

So, what revolutionary, 'anti-social', condemned activity is calling us, as disciples?

2. Jesus and Peter

Maybe Mark can teach us that we are going to get it wrong, but that we are still disciples. Jesus is going to be Son of Man, and he wants us, even if we are still trying to make him into a Messiah. The Spin-off for us is perhaps like this — We initiate something and it seems worthless; but nevertheless someone gets encouraged because of it, and makes progress. We are brought down to earth, but then are set on the way again by an unexpected affirmation 'from the bottom'.

3. Mark's Message to Us

So Mark for us is an 'Up and Downer'. Now and again you'll know you've got it right! Like Jesus, you'll get the sense, 'You are my daughter/son — I am well pleased' (cp. 1:11). Mark, in the end, is a great encourager. Disciples can be down but not out. Followers may follow afar off, but they are still followers. The disciple who is 'down' will get up.

So, what depth are we going to have to reach which will deny the Lord, but through which we will still be disciples?

The end is always 'You are my son', 'You are my daughter', 'You are my disciples today'.

BOOKS

1. On the Gospel of Mark

Paul Achtemeier, *Mark* (SPCK — The Preacher's Bible, 1978).
Very useful on the main themes of Mark.

Morna D. Hooker, *The Message of Mark* (Epworth Press, 1983).
Eight main themes expounded within the first-century context.

Alec McCowen, *Personal Mark* (Hodder paperback, 1985).
An actor reflects on telling the Gospel solo on stage.

Dennis E. Nineham, *Saint Mark* (Penguin Commentaries, rev. ed. 1975).
Useful for much background information.

Eduard Schweizer, *The Good News according to Mark* (SPCK, 1971).
Excellent on the theology and meaning of Mark.

Alec Vidler, *Read, MARK, Learn* (Fount Paperbacks, 1980).
The best and easiest companion for verse-by-verse explanation.

2. Methods of Interpretation

Michel Clévenot, *Materialist Approaches to the Bible* (Orbis Books, USA, 1985).
Has 80 pages of suggestive insights into Mark.

Hans Küng and Jürgen Moltmann, *Conflicting Ways of Interpreting the Bible* (Concilium 138, 1980).
Historical, Critical, Linguistic, Materialistic, Psycho-analytical, Jewish, South American, Black and Feminist Interpreters on Mark 6:45–52.

Hans-Ruedi Weber, *Experiments with Bible Study* (World Council of Churches, 1981).
A fascinating, thorough study, including methods for Mark 2:13–17; 7:31–37; 8:27–38; 10:13–16; 10:32–45; 14:22–25; and 15:20–41.

Walter Wink, *Transforming Bible Study* (SCM Press, 1981).
Psychology and physiology (two sides to the brain) suggest methods which lead to personal change.

3. Jesus in Mark's Gospel

Alan T. Dale, *Portrait of Jesus* (Oxford University Press, 1979).
An easily read, excellent introduction to Jesus' life and work, based mainly on Mark's record.

Albert Nolan, *Jesus Before Christianity: the Gospel of Liberation* (Darton, Longman and Todd, 1977).
Catastrophe, Praxis, Good News and Confrontation in the Gospel.

John J. Vincent, *Radical Jesus* (Marshall Paperbacks, 1986).
The challenge of the Markan Jesus for today's divided Britain.

John J. Vincent, *Secular Christ* (Lutterworth Press, 1968).
A contemporary interpretation of Jesus in Mark's Gospel.

Hans-Ruedi Weber, *Jesus and the Children* (World Council of Churches, 1979).
Markan and other Gospel passages on children, and their power today.

4. Using the Gospel Today

Charles Avila, *Peasant Theology* (Bangkok — East Asian World Student Christian Federation, 1976).
Local people seeing their stories as Gospel-stories.

Ernesto Cardenal, *Love in Practice: The Gospel in Solentiname* (Search Press, 1977).
How Latin American peasants put their action into the Gospel-stories. Further reports in volumes 2, 3 and 4, *The Gospel in Solentiname* (Orbis Books, USA, 1978–79).

John D. Davies, *The Faith Abroad* (Basil Blackwell, Oxford, 1983).
The practical meaning of the model of the Body of Christ.

John D. Davies, *His and Ours* (London: USPG, 1981); *Agenda for Apostles* (1982); *Christ our Life* (1983); *Things of God* (1984); and *Beginning with People* (1985).
Popular courses based on methods similar to those of the present book.

Charles Elliott, *Praying the Kingdom* (Darton, Longman & Todd, 1985).
A striking use of Bible and stories for contemplation and politics.

John Fenton and Michael Hare Duke, *Good News* (SCM Press, 1976).
The 'gospel' is heard as 'new, scandalous, excessive, bringing joy and love'.

John J. Vincent, *Festival for the Future Church* (Ashram Community, 1979).
Mark's stories as signals for future Ministry, Mission, Lifestyle, Politics, Community, etc.

John J. Vincent, *Into the City* (Epworth Press, 1982).
Snaps to Jesus' ministry from Incarnation to Ultimacy, seen in inner-city mission in Sheffield.